GETTING
BEYOND
THE SMALL
TALK

GETTING
BEYOND THE SMALL
TALK

A STEP-BY-STEP APPROACH TO CONVERSATIONAL WITNESSING

BILL D. ROBINSON

OM Publishing
Carlisle, UK

British Library Cataloguing-in-Publication Data.
Robinson, Bill D.
    Getting Beyond the Small Talk:
    Step-by-step Approach to Conversational
    Witnessing. – 2Rev.ed
    I. Title II. Banks, Donald
    269.3

ISBN 1–85078–152–4

OM Publishing is an imprint of Send The Light Ltd,
PO Box 300, Carlisle, Cumbria, CA3 0QS, UK

Typeset by Photoprint, Torquay, Devon
and printed in the UK by Cox and Wyman Ltd, Reading

Contents

Acknowledgments

I would like to thank the following people for their very important contributions to the writing of this book: Clarence Boland, for starting me on my pilgrimage of personal witnessing; Dr. Rick Calenberg for encouraging me to put my thoughts about witnessing into writing; Susan Hofstra (my daughter) for proof-reading my manuscript in its earliest stages; Denise Lindstrom for typing the first draft; Dr. Paul Benware for reviewing the manuscript for accuracy of doctrinal content; Bill Deckard and Terry D. White for their roles in bringing the book to its final form; my two sons, Greg and Eric, for their support and encouragement; and most of all, my wife, Pat – for her many tireless hours at the computer; for her helpful insights on the organization and presentation of my material; for her faithful encouragement through times of discouragement; for being a rock of spiritual strength.

Solomon said there is safety in a multitude of counsellors (Proverbs 11:14). I have certainly been blessed, in this undertaking, by many who have been wise counsellors as well as loyal friends. In anything of lasting worth this book may achieve they have a significant share.

Foreword

This is an enjoyable and helpful little book, which meets a need expressed so often in my visits to church fellowships up and down the country.

At a time when church leaders have turned away from setting up large evangelistic events to local church based evangelism, the stumbling block is too often the failure of church members, not to mention church leaders, to share their faith with their neighbours.

Bill Robinson, with his football pitch imagery, describes the task of witnessing in a way that releases us from much of the fear and guilt that so often accompanies us. Instead of seeing the Christian as the one who must make all the efforts, he looks at the task from both ends, seeing the non-Christian and the Christian gradually coming towards each other in understanding and faith, with responsibility lying with both.

For those enthusiastic about Church Growth, the Engel Scale will come to mind in reading this book. For the average Christian, it will be a real encouragement to go where he has been so afraid to go, the open spaces of faith sharing. It is practical, encouraging and workable.

Read this book, listen to what the Holy Spirit is

saying through it, recognise it is not so much a textbook but a testimony of how the author has journeyed on in his Christian life, then go and be a witness in your community.

John Berry
formerly Evangelism Secretary
Evangelical Alliance

Introduction

John chapter 4 gives the basis for the concept of conversational witnessing. Jesus is speaking to the Samaritan woman at the well. He demonstrates a gentle but straightforward example of how to approach her spiritual need. He moves toward her spiritually through conversation in direct proportion to her yieldedness to spiritual principles and truths. He continues, allowing her limits of understanding and willingness to expand as she responds.

Not only does Jesus set this example early in his ministry, but he goes on to instruct those who would be his disciples to make disciples (Great Commission, Matthew 28:18–20) and to be witnesses (Acts 1:8).

This could all be restated as: We are to be witnesses as we are going through life in order that we will make disciples. As we work and mix with our friends, we should always be looking out for opportunities to witness and make disciples, and thus fulfil our individual part of the Great Commission.

Because it is God's job to convict hearts and save souls, we must be confident that he will lead us to those whom he has prepared. We need not feel guilty if some with whom we share are uninterested or decide to reject the message. Our job is to witness as we go.

In witnessing to people we must remember two facts. One, Christians cannot do the work of convicting a heart or saving a soul. Christians cannot cause the act of regeneration to happen in a person's life.

Two, an unsaved, unregenerate man cannot choose to be saved, to follow Christ, or to love God,

apart from the convicting work of the Holy Spirit in his life. Knowing these two facts can give peace when we consider our part in fulfilling the Great Commission.

This book is designed to share the challenge of witnessing in a proper, effective way. But at the same time, when we witness and people do not respond to God, we must not take it personally or feel guilty.

God's Part

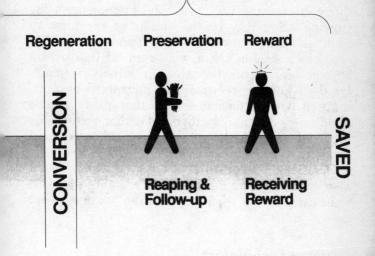

Regeneration   Preservation   Reward

CONVERSION

SAVED

Reaping & Follow-up   Receiving Reward

Effectiveness need not be defined in terms of actual conversions.

God's Network

1 Corinthians 3 displays for us God's pattern of networking – people working together in harmony (not competition) to achieve God's purpose. Some sow, some water, and some reap. But God causes the growth, and each one will receive his reward according to his own labour.

Remember, you may be introducing 'God thoughts' for the very first time in someone's life (sowing). You may be the one he or she turns to again and again for more information on the subject (watering, weeding). You may even see that person become born again through your witness (reaping). Or the whole process may be interrupted by time, location, or circumstances, so that many people (God's network) may be involved in that person's life process before Christ is finally accepted as personal Saviour.

How great and gracious is our God who brings it all together! But we must be faithful and be prepared to be used by him when he tells us to 'witness' as we go.

Causing Discomfort

As I watched the tears well up in the woman's eyes, I began to feel those emotions I had felt before: shame, embarrassment, and humiliation. For I had once again pressed the issue of trusting Christ too far.

She had not responded to my question the way I thought she should. Instead of being sensitive and recognizing her discomfort, I pressed, and she started crying. I was mortified that I had caused such discomfort in someone's life, especially in the spiritual area.

The three of us had come to her house as part of an evangelistic team that visited people on Thursday nights to tell them about the ministries of our church and to talk to them about Christ. We were sitting in her front room as her guests. What had started as a pleasant visit to share Christ turned into a disaster. She said something about trusting Christ and her own works for her eternal hope. I had pressed her, explaining that our hope is in Christ alone. I thought I was being polite.

Then, when the tears started, I asked what the problem was. She told of her confusion and discomfort from our visit. I apologized and tried my best to soothe her. How do you leave graciously after causing a situation like that? With mixed emotions, I apologized again and we left, our New Testaments hanging heavy in our pockets.

The Dinner Guests

Once I shared Christ with a milkman and eventually he made a profession of faith. I knew that in order to be really effective in reaching people for Christ I needed to get involved in their lives. So to reach out to his wife and family, my wife and I decided to have them over for dinner.

All went well, for the most part. I deliberately did

not talk about spiritual things. If they came up in the conversation, I would respond. I do not remember exactly what I said but, as they were getting ready to leave, the milkman's wife came back to me very firmly with, 'Bill, we are very happy at our church and do not have any intention of leaving it to join your church.'

After I recovered from her direct method of dealing with an intruder, I explained that I was not trying to get them to leave their church to join ours. I was simply telling what a difference Christ had made in my life. Apparently that made them feel I had a 'better-than-thou' attitude. As I tried to talk my way out of this bad situation, they excused themselves and left. I spent the rest of the evening wishing I could remove my foot from my mouth.

The 'Good-Old-Boy' Electrician

I first met Jim at work when he came to fix some plugs. He came in talking. He was one of those honest, down-to-earth types, friendly and easy-going. I was drawn to him immediately, and felt very comfortable with him. We developed a rapport quickly. Jim was excited about his skills as an electrician and he loved to talk about his work. By this time God had brought me a long way in my witnessing experience and I was developing some tact in my methods, or so I thought.

As I grew to know Jim better, I laid down some 'bridge work' (building bridges to people in order to earn the right to share Christ). Jim never hesitated or withdrew. But as I look back, I can see he was not as excited talking about the things of Christ as he was about discussing his electrician's skills. I assumed that was happening simply because people often are reluctant to discuss subjects about which they know little.

As I shared with Jim over a period of months he came to the point of praying and professing Christ. I took him through an immediate follow-up lesson and taught him about assurance. He answered all the questions correctly.

At this point, I always try to bring in a third party to help establish in the new Christian's mind what an important transaction has just taken place in his life. Hopefully, I can do it with some Christian he knows. Often I call my wife, Pat, into the 'new birth' situation, and she always congratulates the new Christian with a welcome into the family.

I did this with Jim. Pat reassured him of the importance of what had just taken place in his life. On this particular occasion there was another Christian in the building to whom Pat introduced Jim. She also welcomed him in a warm, friendly way, and Jim responded by talking about his religious background. Although not really excited over what had just taken place, he agreed with our statements about Christ's forgiveness, God's love, and spiritual and eternal things.

Before Jim left, I showed him where to read in God's Word for assurance and discussed the importance of praying regularly. He thanked me and left. I was excited and could hardly wait for Jim's next visit so we could share again. I wanted to watch his newfound faith becoming real to him.

But I never saw Jim again. Maybe his work took him elsewhere. He could have moved further away or changed jobs, which would have made it inconvenient for him to return. But it may be that Jim did not want to discuss his personal spiritual life. Maybe his conversion was just because he did not want to offend me by refusing. I may never know.

I have started this book with what may seem, to some, to be failures. These are not my only negative encounters in sharing Christ. Negative experiences were, and are, my training ground. God is using situations like these to make me more sensitive and to teach me his ways.

I tell them hoping that others who have had negative experiences sharing Christ can receive some hope and encouragement in learning some of the ideas and concepts contained in this book.

Dilemma

There is danger in not knowing how to witness properly:

1. We may stop because of discouragement.
2. We may press the person to make a decision and thereby cause problems in our relationship.
3. A person may appear to trust Christ because of our badgering, which results in profession, not possession.

There are many books on the subject of witnessing. Most are written to challenge people to witness, or they stress the biblical commands to witness. But not much is written on how to witness effectively, especially over a long period of time, to a given person.

This short book is not an all-inclusive manual on witnessing, nor is it an exhaustive work on the subject. It is simply an attempt to share what has worked in my life over and over. Because of my love for people and my desire to share Christ with them, I was motivated to develop a way of witnessing which is as effective as possible without being offensive.

1

An Overview of the "Football Field" Method

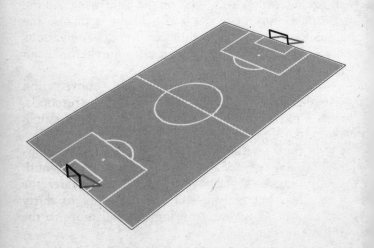

In 1 Corinthians 3:6–8 the apostle Paul talks about planting, watering, reaping, and reward. Saved and unsaved alike are in a process. Dr. Howard Hendricks of Dallas Theological Seminary says that people are in a process of coming to know the Lord and we must plug into that process wherever they are. Has someone already sown the gospel in this person's life? Is it time to water?

A Field With Two Ends

In order to determine where God has brought people in their spiritual process, I visualize myself on a spiritual football field. I am on the right wing. All the rest of the team are there to help me. I picture the other person in his goal mouth. I have to use various means to get the ball much closer to him before I can shoot for goal.

The first ten metres is general conversation (weather, football, cricket, whatever). If he responds, then I move forward with talk about our personal interests (family, job, and so on).

My third level of conversation is general religious talk (churches, Sunday school, family services, youth group activities, and so forth). We are nearer the goal area, but we are still about twenty to thirty metres out. It is time to bring the ball more to the middle of the field.

I move to personal religious comments, concerning

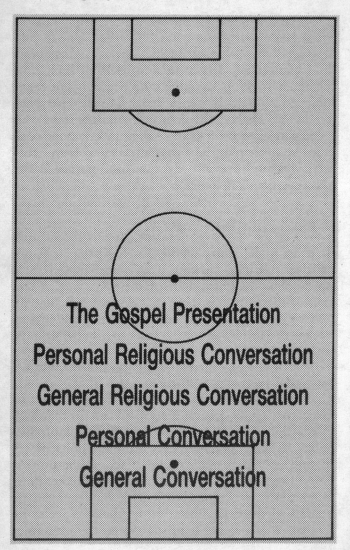

The Gospel Presentation

Personal Religious Conversation

General Religious Conversation

Personal Conversation

General Conversation

myself and concerning him. I will go from talking about God generally to what Christ has done for me or what he means to me. I will go from talking about the decline of morals generally to what the Bible says specifically. All along, I have been asking for feedback, and now I begin asking more personal questions about his views regarding his church, if he goes to one, the Bible and Christ. I am now only eighteen metres out, on the edge of the penalty area.

Throughout we have only moved forward if the person has been responding by talking, following, or involving himself in the conversation and the direction it has been going.

Now it is time to shoot for goal and start the gospel presentation. At this point, I take it steady and I do not want to rush things. It is at this crucial time that many muff their opportunity.

Of course, this is also where our football analogy breaks down. The other person is no longer a goalkeeper trying to keep me out. If he is ready to trust the Lord Jesus Christ, he no longer confronts me, but wants to turn in a new direction so that we can shoot for goal together!

My motivation in all this is not to convict him of his sin or to save a soul. Only God can do that. My motivation is twofold. First, I want to be a witness to an unbeliever of the things Christ has done in my own life. Second, I wish to see where in the process God has brought him and to discover whether he is interested in the things of God.

If the "big picture" of this approach is seen, the tension in witnessing will be reduced tremendously.

The average person's view of witnessing is as follows:

First, in much of Christianity there is confusion between soul-winning and witnessing. I believe the average Christian thinks he or she has to save souls. But our responsibility is to witness; God's business is to save the soul.

Second, because of this confusion, that same average Christian imagines that he has to rush down the entire football field, brushing aside all opposition, and shoot for goal every time. He is in too much of a hurry and he starts pressing the other person far too quickly with the gospel, the Christian life, and his subject's sinful condition. Eventually he gets discouraged because he either gets nowhere, or the abruptness provokes a negative reaction.

At this crucial stage of the witnessing process, one must watch for subtleties of expression which can take on many forms: physical, verbal, and emotional. Emotions can be expressed in the body by raising or lowering eyebrows. The mouth may be tightened in a nervous smile or frown; a jaw may be firmly set, or a foot may begin jerking up and down. Keep your eyes open for these small things: they are important indicators of how a person is feeling. The whole nervous system can be showing through that tapping foot. So it pays to be observant.

A young lady walked into the firm where I work. I glanced up, smiled, and said, "Good morning." In all, I saw her for only about ten seconds. After finishing my work, I approached her. "Are you having a bad day?" I asked. She immediately broke into tears and poured out her heart. My wife had been with her that hour and had not picked up on her "down countenance." She said to me later, "How do you do that?" I watch and listen for sights and sounds with my eyes and ears, and I sense emotions in my spirit. Allow your spirit to reach out to another's spirit. Be sensitive and quiet as you observe someone who is wounded or upset.

Verbal expressions can come in words, in voice tones, and in the pitch of the voice. When we hear negative words of complaining, self-pity, anger, bitterness, or a wounded spirit, it is a sign of inner trouble. When talking on the phone, for example, notice how you can be frustrated by the way the person on the other end pitches the voice. Take the opportunity to ask, "How are things going today?" I do this, and it often relaxes a person so I get much better results.

In witnessing we can learn to listen for voice tones to determine whether or not we should reach out. Witnessing may follow naturally, or you may sense that the timing is not right and simply minister to the hurt in that life. There have been times when I have brought up the subject of spiritual things and have immediately seen that the people have become uncomfortable. They have looked away or they have started straightening the room. Be sensitive to subtleties of expression which indicate the time to speak and the time to refrain.

You see, our first important job is *discovery*. We need to discover just where the person is and, in doing that, "let him be." Relax and enjoy the person while discovering where God has him in the spiritual process. We need not feel the pressure of trying to force him to some point on the football field. Most of us did not respond to the gospel the very first time we heard it.

I enjoy discovery. I go to a shopping centre with my wife, Pat. While she is enjoying herself shopping, I will go and sit down on a bench to see if God is going to send someone my way. When an individual sits down next to me I start the discovery process.

I am ready to shoot for goal immediately. But that is seldom the way it is in real life. When the conversation begins, I start the process of discovery. Just how far the person will progress depends on where God has brought him thus far, and how responsive he is to the things I say. If the person opens up to me, I respond. But if he does not, I assume he is not ready. I do not want to be offensive by pushing ahead. This may be the wrong time, wrong place, or maybe he does not yet trust me. Unlike real football, I do not push people around the field. It is exciting just to find out or to discover where the person's spiritual life is at the moment.

With the "football field" method I see two areas of responsibility, one on each end of the field.

My Responsibility

The first responsibility has to do with the sixty-five metres separating me from the man in the goal mouth – my sixty-five metres, I call them. My approach needs to be wise – based on the wisdom God gives. To be an effective witness we must:

1. Have a Plan

Do you know from Scripture what happened to you in the process of coming to the Lord Jesus Christ? If so, share that. There are all kinds of classes, books, audio and video tapes that can help you. Read and memorize Scripture. But basically, tell your story, weaving the gospel clearly into your discussion.

2. Stay Alert

When I join a group which trains people to share their faith, I find myself being more alert about witnessing. Like anything else, if it gets low priority, it will not be attended to properly. Sometimes instead of being alert we just stay "busy" and never get the job done. In our home we call that "opening the mail." An example is the salesperson in the office, whose job is to get on the phone and make appointments in order to make sales. One of the hardest aspects of selling is getting on the phone to call someone who does not want to talk to you. It is known as "call reluctance."

So what does the salesman do? He comes in about 9:30, gets a cup of coffee, talks a little to others, then the mail comes in. He cannot get to the phone now because he has to "open the mail." After doing all this, he checks the time and it is about 11:15. Too close to lunchtime! He stays busy, but he really is not making any money.

Christians "open the mail" by reading, discussing, and taking classes on sharing their faith. But they often avoid actual witnessing. Stay alert for signs people are throwing your way. Look for opportunities to probe peoples' lives for their needs and hurts and where they are in God's process. Do not procrastinate. Begin to share the Good News!

3. Use Tact

I once was witnessing to a doctor from a local university. I thought he was open to our conversation until he said, "Bill, I'd rather take off all my clothes and run down the street naked than talk about religion." (A Christian psychiatrist could probably do a whole workshop on that statement!) We must be careful not to offend people.

A dictionary definition of tact is "a keen sense of what to say or do in order to maintain good relations with others or avoid offending." When it comes to sharing something about which we feel open and free we must remember that the gospel is convicting and can be disturbing. People are burdened with sin. When we start probing around, doing "open heart surgery" with our questions, we may touch an exposed nerve. That can hurt deeply, and we may be confronted with all sorts of reactions.

I taught a class of young married people at church one Sunday morning. The topic was on being an effective witness and using tact. So to get their attention and to make my point, my opening remark was a question. I asked, "Well, how was everyone's sex life this past week?" It was funny to see the uncomfortable body language: people turning red, looking down at the floor, and a few laughing nervously.

I proceeded to share with them the point that religious life, to some people, is a very personal, private affair, something like a couple's sex life.

There are times I do not talk to people about their personal religious life just as I would not inquire into their sex life. It's too personal! Some people will not open up until bridges have been built. Friendships need to be established. You have to earn the right to ask personal questions.

4. Be Faithful

I remember one night when we were in the visitation part of our training session and visited a family in their home. The mother was especially interested in our discussions. On either our first or second visit one of our team members presented the gospel. The mother was not ready to trust Christ that night, but we found out later her teenage son, who was sitting there with us, went into his room after we left and gave his life to Christ. We did not press the mother for a decision. We chatted generally and then left. But we continued to pray for her. The mother accepted Christ as her Saviour some time later.

Many years afterwards I was with my wife in a supermarket and I heard someone call out my name. It was this same woman. She immediately started thanking me for our visit. She said they were still attending church and were very happy in the Lord.

I believe sometimes the process of being faithful in witnessing is pictured as: (*a*) being at a certain place at a certain time, or (*b*) forging ahead, not stopping. Faithfulness can also be explained by using the football field analogy. Being faithful doesn't always mean proceeding down the field. Maybe being faithful means slowing down. If I detect something that warns me the person does not want to hear what I am sharing, it takes a real act of faith for me to be quiet and back away.

Why do we feel unfaithful just because we use tact? It is not that we do not want to share Christ. The problem is that our subject does not want to hear the gospel and is telling us so. I must defer and trust that God will use even my restraint to help bring that person to himself. When we use tact and trust God to "give the increase" (1 Corinthians 3:7), we do not bruise the potential fruit. Then, later, if another Christian witnesses and has more of an open door, that person might be more responsive to a witness because I was not obnoxious or aggravating. This is depending on God's network of Christian people to get the task completed.

I first met Denny when he came into my place of business. While he was there I started my casual probing to get to know him, and to build some bridges. In my questioning, I discovered that he and his wife, Sue, had just moved into the area. When I talk with such a person, I first ask whether he has discovered all the services in town including the town hall, fire station, police station, and so on. Then I ask if he has any special interests and would like to join any of the local clubs. Finally, I ask if he has found a place of worship.

In this case, Denny said he was attending a church some thirty-five to forty minutes from his home. It was the same denomination as the church I attended, so I suggested he might like to visit our church. I mentioned that it would save driving time. He admitted that sounded like a good idea.

After they had visited our church several times,

one of our evangelism teams went to their house. Denny was a Christian but Sue was not. That night she trusted Christ as her Saviour. They both became growing Christians and are living for the Lord today. When Denny's parents came to town to visit them, they wanted to meet this businessman who had told Denny and Sue about the church where their daughter-in-law had come to know the Lord. I was just doing what I love to do, but from their point of view, this was God's network in action.

The parents had believed that when their children moved out of town to a strange area, they were leaving the only Christian influence in their lives. But God had their children right in the palm of his hand! By using his network, God brought Denny and Sue to himself. Nobody else gets the credit; he did it. The sovereign God uses faithful witnesses to accomplish his purposes. That belief frees me from guilt when I feel the need to back away when sharing my faith.

Remember that the majority of people are not going to let you get anywhere near the goal area. Christ said, in Matthew 7, "Narrow is the way to life, and few enter ... and broad is the way to destruction and many will enter there" (author's paraphrase). So I know that the farther down the field I go, the fewer people I get to talk to about the Lord. In order to have any "life message" at all, I must learn restraint. Some people will stay open, but I must do more backing off than advancing. Many people do not mind a Christian believing for himself, but they do not want him to talk to them about it, or to personalize it to them.

There is a time to go forward, being faithful. There is also a faithfulness in holding off. The wise person knows when to do each.

5. Have the Right Attitude

In all this I am not talking about having a "bag of tricks." I mean, instead, being faithful to the task God has given me and bringing glory to him in everything I do.

If the person to whom we are witnessing rejects our Lord and then we, in turn, reject that person, we are not playing fairly. If I cannot get the individual to do what I want him to do through some sort of manipulation, and if in turn I reject him, then I have ruined the message of love.

According to Scripture, we are ambassadors for Christ. An ambassador takes a message from one king and delivers it to another. If the receiving king rejects the message, the ambassador shouldn't take it personally. The same applies to us. We are ambassadors for Christ. When someone misunderstands our intent and becomes negative or unkind, we must not take it personally. We should pray, love, and remain open to that person.

I knew a young man who was fairly active in his church's youth group. We would talk about "religious" things and eventually I was able to move into the personalized area with him. I made a lunch appointment with him in order to explain the gospel more completely. Because of our previous discussions, I believed he would want to hear this "Good News."

But after sharing the gospel, I sensed his indifference. He was busy in his work and he became less interested in church activities. A few years later he opened a bar and disco. He still patronized our business, so occasionally I would bring up general religious subjects to see whether he would allow further discussions. But he only grew more indifferent. Pat and I remain open and friendly to him. We still pray for him and trust that God's network will complete his will in our friend's life.

In this section we have been talking about the witness's responsibility. Now let us talk about what is going on at the other end of the field.

The Receiver's Responsibility

The receiver's first responsibility is to listen to my witness; if he chooses to listen, it is because God is working. We must realize we are not responsible for what he does at his end of the field. We need to recognise our limitations and trust God to work in his heart. If we push too hard we can put him off wanting to hear anything about Jesus.

His second area of responsibility concerns his will. It is his responsibility before God to choose. If he chooses not to respond to the promptings of the Holy Spirit, he will have to answer for that.

I often see Christians badgering relatives about their unresponsive attitudes toward God. The Christian feels that if he just says the right thing, just one more time, then maybe this new insight he has gained from a sermon might help change Aunt Mabel. Just one more tract, one more sermonette might do the job. We believe the problem is that the unsaved relative does not have enough information. If only we could get more of the Bible to her or in her. . . . Oh, how we must drive our relatives nuts!

The fact is, your relatives may not like God or want him in their lives. Romans 5:10 explains that your unsaved relative is an enemy of God. It isn't a matter of not being able to believe. It is a matter of not *wanting* to believe. In Romans 3, Paul says the whole world is guilty before God. There is none who seeks after God. People *will* not to be saved. Even if you argue that a person came to know the Lord after being witnessed to for years, it was still *God* who made the difference.

When unsaved relatives see Christian loved ones coming, they often perceive them as unwanted salesmen. "Oh, no. All I'm going to hear about this afternoon is their product!" Why can't we just settle down and be human with loved ones? After we have been a verbal witness, we need to be quiet and be a life witness.

My wife's mother, who was a Christian, died when Pat was only thirteen. Pat was the oldest of five children, and at age fourteen she invited Christ into her life. Knowing that her mother was already a Christian, she had a passion to share that experience with her brothers and sisters and her father. They listened. Some responded. Dad, however, made it very clear that religion was a personal matter — between the person and God. "You have no right to ask!" was his sentiment. She simply told him it was important to her to know that they would share eternity together. He said, "Just don't you worry about it!" End of discussion.

All we could do was to pray for him, letting our lives demonstrate the love of God, and looking for openings to witness again. Thirty years later Pat's father did trust Christ as Saviour. His salvation was a thrilling conversion and we are so grateful to the Lord.

It is necessary to keep praying and keep trusting God. Just remember that the response must come from the person. They are the ones who need to make the decision. Do not feel guilty if they do not, but be prepared if they do.

My Attitude Toward the Response

A person's response will be the result of God, the Holy Spirit, working in his or her life. Let us picture two individuals walking away from God. They both hear the truth that "whosoever shall call upon the name of the Lord shall be saved" (Romans 10:13). One stops, turns around, and comes after Christ. Why did one turn and the other keep going his or her own way? It was the Holy Spirit's convicting power that made the difference.

When I have had the opportunity to share the gospel with someone, it was not me who changed that person's life. It was God, the Holy Spirit, who brought the truth to that sinful heart. Any spiritual progress that person makes during our conversation has little to do with my plans, study, memorization, tact, or faithfulness; it is made only because of the Holy Spirit's working. True, we have our part, but that part is insignificant compared to the greater work God is doing in the individual's heart. Anyone can share, pray, listen, be tactful, and be faithful. If I am not doing those things, God will use someone else and I will miss the blessing. Only God can change the heart.

Consider the analogy of a garden. It is Spring and we go out and plant some seeds. We fertilize the seeds, water them, and we hoe and weed. A few weeks later some green shoots come up from the ground. Then we say, "Look what we did." Wrong! We did what was expected, but it was God who did the greater work. Making a green plant come from a little seed was not our doing. The Almighty Power who does this is the same Power who woos a person to himself.

This concept was very frustrating to me. My work? God's work? When do I work? When does God's work take over? I began to understand when I saw that it all comes down to trust and praise.

First, I realized I do not have to trust my own efforts in witnessing. I need not be concerned that I forgot a point in an evangelism outline, or fouled up quoting a Bible verse, or that in my ignorance I pressed a person too hard and caused alienation. I must put my trust in God's greater work.

I had been witnessing for a number of years when we started a church outreach programme. On our first visit with my initial trainees, I encountered a lady who said she did not believe she sinned very much. I was so taken aback I could not think of what to say. I quoted some arguments about sin and sinners. After we left and were driving back to the church, I was reminded of Romans 3:23 and 6:23.

"For all have sinned and come short of the glory of God," and "For the wages of sin is death but the gift of God is eternal life through Jesus Christ our Lord."

I could not believe I had forgotten the basic Scriptures in my answer to her! I grieved over that failure for years. I often worried that she would not have another chance to hear those two Bible verses and that somehow I was going to be held responsible for that failure.

But God will take even my mistakes, especially when I am attempting to be faithful, and make the most of them for his glory. It is God who brings the plant forth, and it will be God who brings that person along the process to salvation. I must trust him to do that. I must not focus on my mistakes. This is no excuse for lack of preparation, but once you have prepared yourself or are in the process of preparing yourself to have an effective witness, then you must not punish yourself unnecessarily for occasional mistakes. Still, repeated mistakes call for reflection to see where your presentation may be sharpened. Strengthen your weak areas so you do not bring reproach on the Lord through ineptness.

The second area of understanding is praise. It comes from trusting God. The praise goes to God, who can do more than I ever thought. When I compare what my responsibility is to what God does in man's heart, there is no doubt where the praise belongs. You will know this praise when you see someone to whom you have been witnessing accept Christ, start to attend church, and grow in their Christian walk. Remember, things take time.

One busy day at work the phone rang. I answered it and heard, "Bill, this is Ron. I want to drop by and share some of the things that have happened to me. I am now pastoring a small church." After a short conversation, I hung up the phone and as I waited for Ron, I reminisced about our first meeting. He had been a customer of mine before I knew how to witness. We always enjoyed our times together. So, when I started sharing what Christ had done in my life, he was a natural target for witness.

I recalled that he had some problems with the "person of Christ," as to who he was. Being new at witnessing, I asked permission to bring my pastor over to his house. The evening we visited, the pastor was going through the gospel when Ron asked his question. The pastor answered it. After hearing the gospel in its entirety, Ron bowed his head and trusted Christ. His concern about who Christ was had been answered and just melted away. Ron started attending our church with his family. He eventually joined another church and many years later decided to go to college and then into the ministry.

Ron's phone call came at a time when I was facing some real struggles. Hearing about his continuing on with the Lord and going into the ministry was a real encouragement to me. It was a strong reinforcement of what witnessing is all about. When you see a person growing in Christ and you know you had a small part in that life, you wonder that an infinite God can use such a finite instrument to help in the great act of heart regeneration.

1. Give God Time

I remember talking to a man about the things of Christ. He prayed and made a "profession." I shared some follow-up materials. But he just sat there. I do not know to this day whether he actually trusted Christ or not. It could be he just "performed a religious act."

But now his son, who is in his early twenties, is asking questions about television preachers and man's relationship with God. Interestingly, I never brought up the subject to him. He probably knew of the conversations between his dad and me, and they prompted a stirring in his soul. Now he is asking some very significant questions. It seems he is responding to the seed that was sown in his dad seven or eight years earlier. It is exciting to see a person start to be spiritually awakened. I look forward to sharing Christ with him.

2. Learn to Live With Tension

Witnessing brings tension and Christians must learn to live with it. Let me illustrate.

I remember a family to whom I tried to witness when they were going through an incredibly difficult time. I had known the two brothers (we will call them Jim and Tom) since they were at secondary school. They were pleasant, easy-going, good-looking lads. We always had enjoyed general conversation. One day Jim called, asking me to visit his brother in the hospital. Tom had been at a bar one night and had become involved in an argument with another customer. It was only something trivial, but a brawl broke out. The other man pulled out a knife and stabbed Tom. He was rushed by ambulance to hospital in a critical state.

As I stood at Tom's bedside, looking down at this tragic result of a senseless act, my heart broke. In the thirty minutes I was there we progressed to personalized spiritual conversation. In a situation like this people are often willing to listen. But as I explained the gospel I did not sense any spiritual response from Tom. He agreed with me, but did not seem to personalize anything I had shared with him.

On the way home I explained to Jim what I had said to Tom. He, too, was "polite" concerning my religion but showed no significant interest. I had never met the parents before. Shortly after this event, however, the father came into our business, willing to talk about some of the struggles he was presently facing. The mother, I learned, was an alcoholic who had moved out of the home some years earlier. As the father shared, he was moved to tears. I tried to console him and I told him of God's love. (Avoid stock answers and remarks at a time like this. Simply empathize and love.) However, he, too, was indifferent. I saw Jim only one time after that. Tom died.

When people go through hard times and do not seem to respond to God's love, it can create real inner tension for the Christian who wants to share the love of Christ. We must learn to live with that. Tragedies cause tension, and if a Christian comes alongside and tries to share the gospel, that can cause still more discomfort for the suffering person. For this reason we must be very sensitive in how we witness at crisis times. Perhaps the sufferer has turned to you because you are the only source of spiritual comfort he or she has. Guard against high expectations of leading a person to Christ in this situation. Simply love and help as best you can.

There are several tensions you may face, such as: (1) Knowing how far you should go down the field and when you should stop; and (2) Seeing dearly loved friends and relatives not trusting Christ and not being able to say any more to them about the gospel. We must love and enjoy people even when they choose to reject our witness and tell us that they are not really interested.

In this state of not being able to say any more, we must learn to hurt and pray. We hurt because we love them so much even though they reject Christ. We pray for wisdom and watch for new opportunities. Our patience, attitudes, and actions may communicate the love of Christ more effectively than our words. Show love by reaching out with "love-works." You can speak volumes with any little kindness or act of consideration, such as gifts, cards, meals, and visits (1 Corinthians 13).

In 1 Corinthians 3:6–8, Paul talks about planting, watering, growing, and reward. I like that analogy. It takes the pressure off. Depending on where the person is in the process, I sometimes plant and I sometimes water. But what is so calming to my spirit is that I do not have to cause the growth. God is going to reward me for the lesser work of planting and watering. Just watching the process of regeneration is enough thrill and reward.

2

Kicking Off –
General Conversation

Salesmen really interested in selling will watch a parade and see not only the parade, but potential customers. That is the attitude a successful salesman must have in order to do his prospecting. Certain steps must be followed to make the sale.

In the same way, we Christians should see everyone we meet as potential candidates for the Kingdom of God. We should be asking ourselves where God has each person in the salvation process, and how we should fit into the plan. Will God use me today to witness to this individual? Just how interested is this person in the things of God? Is he like the Ethiopian whom Philip dealt with, or is she like the woman at the well whom Christ had to gently persuade and convince before she believed? The person might be like King Agrippa to whom Paul witnessed. He was open to hearing about Christ, even though he did not become a Christian at that time. We need to assess each individual's 'spiritual pilgrimage' as we converse in a general way.

Doors of Interest

In a game of football, the forwards are looking for 'gaps' in the other team's defensive line. Likewise, when engaged in general conversation, we look for doors that might be used to gain entrance into a specific area of interest. I try different subjects. For example, if we have already had general conversation and I want to move to more personalized subjects, I may try talking about the individual's occupation. But maybe he hates his work, and responds to me with silence or aggravation, and so I drop the subject. I might switch to discussing his family. I need to search for a contact point.

Imagine two sticks of dynamite. One has a long, wet fuse. The other has a short, dry fuse. If I tried to light the long, wet one, I would do so without success. It would take for ever to ignite the dynamite. On the other hand, the stick with the short, dry fuse might go off before I could drop it. It is the same with people. With some, you may talk and talk to them and they do not respond. But with others you may say very little, and they are off and talking.

We need to establish subjects of common interest that might lead to a discussion of the things of Christ. To illustrate, remember again Christ's example in John 4. Jesus began by talking about water, but ultimately discussed the condition of the woman's spiritual life.

The best-equipped Christians have knowledge in a number of subject areas. Do not be an ignorant Christian! Learn to be an interesting conversationalist, fortified with information both secular and religious:

Secular

1. Watch the evening news or listen to comprehensive radio news broadcasts.

2. Read at least the front section of the daily newspaper or a summary of the news in brief. Know

at least a little about current events on the national and local level so you can speak intelligently about them.

3. **Attend lectures, seminars, concerts,** football matches, so that you are able to carry on a conversation on a variety of subjects.

Religious

1. **Know the Bible's position** on controversial issues. Regular study of the Word is imperative.

2. **Know your own position** on issues, based on the Bible. Be sure you can state what you believe, not because of what your parents and/or church believe, but because of the convictions you have arrived at biblically on your own before God. You need to know, for example, what Scripture you would use to challenge an agnostic in a discussion of the deity of Christ.

3. **Subscribe to magazines** that deal with current events and issues from a Christian perspective, so you can speak knowledgeably concerning your biblical position.

4. **Read books by Christian authors** about other religions and cults so you will know what they believe and why they believe it. I once had an employee who was offended when I accepted the Book of Mormon from a door-to-door representative. But the reason I did it was to get the facts from the Mormons' own source regarding certain doc-

trinal positions. If an army commander could get his hands on the other side's strategy plan that would be valuable information!

Most unsaved people who attend church are unaware of the heresy that exists in the cults. When talking to a person whose church or religion believes in the deity of Christ and a cult is mentioned which I know does not so believe, I make it a point to state that fact. Just being knowledgeable about such an issue and stating it demonstrates your interest in and awareness of religious beliefs and could lead to conversation concerning the person's need of Christ.

Note that when you are making a biblical point it is not always necessary to quote the Bible word for word, putting it in the King James style of *thees* and *thous* and stating where that verse is found. Sometimes I reword the verse, putting it in my own words in a conversational style. For example, when speaking about an atheist, I will say, 'An atheist is without excuse. Creation, itself, testifies of God's existence.' ('For the invisible things of him from the creation of things that are made, even his eternal power and Godhead: so that they are without excuse' [Romans 1:20].) Sometimes I make an 'intellectual quote,' as if I were quoting Plato or Aristotle. But I will quote Jesus or Paul: 'But Jesus Christ said, "I am the way" ' (John 14:6).

Probing Two Ways

It is helpful to probe the person at least two ways: in the areas of interest and knowledge.

Many people fail to probe their subject's areas of interest. They are so busy and interested in themselves that they do not care about other peoples' interests. Next time you are in a group, notice how infrequently people ask others about their interests. Be interested enough in the answers that you will later be able to reflect back with them about some interest they have mentioned.

I am a 'Disney freak' according to my friends. I love the theme parks Disneyland and Walt Disney World, and know a lot of trivia about them. When designing the parks, some of the consultants were concerned that if they constructed the buildings three stories high on Main Street, they would be too tall and would not look as quaint as they desired. Walt Disney conceived the idea of pushing the buildings down, or limiting the height by using a technique he called 'forced perspective.' They made the first floor of each building 90 percent of its normal height, the second floor 70 percent of its normal height, and the third floor 60 percent. That way the buildings look normal, and yet the spectator gets more of a feeling of fantasy – a 'dolls house' effect.

Another interesting bit of trivia involves the names on the windows. They are named after people from the Disney organization, either past or present.

I have shared these and a few other facts about Disney with people who I knew were going to America and would probably be visiting Disneyland. Many of them have told me that as they were strolling down Main Street they thought of some of the things I had told them and that this had contributed to their enjoyment of the experience.

Probing Knowledge

Have you ever, when lost, asked a person how to find a certain place? Oh, how they love to explain all the left and right hand turns! People love giving directions. Asking for information can be an excellent way of starting a conversation. I love asking older people questions about life. There is much to be learned from them. If we would take the time to probe people's interests and experiences, we would be amazed at what they know, for most people are bursting at the seams to talk. I suspect that when my wife and I get together with friends, they must say to each other, 'Remember not to say anything in front of Bill about Disney!'

If you want to really be good at probing people, here is an exercise to try. The next time you are with someone, do not make any statements about yourself or your interests. Delve into the other person's interests and experiences by asking questions. Spend about thirty minutes a day doing this. You may be frustrated at first, but you will see mutual interests evolve and opportunities for witness develop.

No Ulterior Motives

Be a good conversationalist for the sake of conversation itself – just to be and to make a friend. Don't try to be a good conversationalist for the sole reason of eventually sharing Christ. That is a dead-end street. People will sense the phoniness. It will only frustrate you. Always trying to steer the conversation toward the things of Christ can be clumsy and awkward, lacking ease and social grace. And it can create a sense of failure when the unsaved person is not following the lead.

When we try various comments in a probing way to discover where the person is in God's process and that person does not respond, then we must relax. We must be able to continue in general conversation without feeling guilty about not being able to manipulate the direction. Relax and enjoy the conversation and the person even if you never get the opportunity to say something about Christ. Even if the individual eventually rejects all witness of Christ, I still want to remain their friend. Too many times when people reject the message of Christ, Christians, in turn, reject the unbeliever. This ought not to be, for it creates a negative image of Christians as scalp-hunters who care little for people.

1. Listen intently to people

Be genuine. I attend a large church. On occasion we have had some 'Christian celebrities' to preach. But often when talking with them personally, you get the feeling they would rather be talking to someone else who is more important than you, or they make body movements or gestures to end the thirty-to-forty-second conversation. When talking to people, give them your undivided attention. Look them in the eye; talk to them – not at or around them.

I remember walking into our church hall during our Missionary Weekend and I saw the guest speaker sitting at the front. He was one of the 'top men' in a particular missionary society and extremely well-known. I did not want to bother him, and so as I greeted him and shook his hand I kept moving slowly. What a pleasant surprise to have him hold on to my hand so that I had to stop and talk with him. I could tell from his face that he wanted to talk. His ministry and position in the mission had not got in the way of his remaining interested in ordinary people, something which can very easily happen.

2. Do not interrupt

Let people not only finish their sentences but also their complete thoughts. If they do get interrupted, help by bringing the conversation back to them by asking, 'What was it you were saying about . . . ?'

3. Set the tone of the conversation

If I encounter an offensive person, immediately I want to establish who I am and what I stand for. Sometimes in newly developing relationships a negative mindset may develop. If a dominant personality begins with bad language or vulgar stories, I waste no time countering this behaviour by offering something to offset it.

A few years ago I visited an Army camp. While in the mess hall for a cup of coffee, I encountered some vile language. When only males are present the language in the Armed Services can become really bad. But, whenever I was able to be with one or two of these same men alone, I would take charge of the situation right up front by dropping 'God talk' into the conversation. That is, I would start filtering into our discussion the general religious talk – religious jokes, or stories about church activities or church football games I had organised. If people can be ignorant and vile without embarrassment, why should I be timid about my convictions? Put in positive words for God.

4. Be ready to move the conversation to a deeper level

As I have general conversation with people, I am looking for those items of a personal nature about which I can be specific. I am looking and moving towards the area of personalized conversation.

3

First Ten Metres –
Personal
Conversation

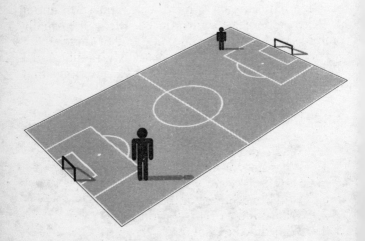

The objective at this level is to get to know an individual on a more personal level – to become a friend. When we become friends, it is easier to introduce people to our Friend of Friends.

Listen With Care

Many of the principles from the previous chapter may be followed. In general conversation, we must listen for those subjects which will give insights into the person's life and interests. Once something of a personal nature is mentioned, ask a question about it. When a subject is introduced, there are usually multiple spin-offs that can come out of that.

For example, if a person says, 'My family and I went camping this past week,' the questions that could issue from that remark are:

1. Did you have fun?
2. How many members are in your family?
3. Where did you go?
4. What do you like best about camping?
5. How long were you gone?
6. How long have you been camping?
7. What kind of tent do you have?
8. Who did the cooking?
9. Was the weather good?

Depending on the answers you get, you can also develop a multiple list of follow-up questions.

Upon being reunited with a friend you have not seen for some time, ask about life in an overview, systematic way. It is so uplifting for a friend to tell you what has been happening over the years. Ask:

1. How have you been?
2. How are your wife and children?
3. How are your mother and dad?
4. How is your work life?
5. What has been going on at your church?

We can apply these principles with new friends as well. Probe into their life with a shortened list of questions, but not with just 'How have you been?' 'Oh, fine. How have you been?' Cliché questions usually bring cliché answers. Use creative questions and look people in the eye.

Care enough to remember. Take the time to get facts correct and store up your knowledge of what has been shared so you can ask about it later. This shows genuine love and concern and is uplifting to the recipient. My wife is so impressed with those who have done this with her, that she has incorporated it into her own conversations.

Get to know a person by asking questions about:

1. The past – birthplace, family, education, and work.
2. The present – family, work, education, interests, and hobbies.
3. The future – goals, plans, retirement, and objectives.

What Are They Interested In?

Ask about areas of expertise such as:

1. Musical instruments
2. Artistic abilities
3. Hobbies, such as carpentry or crafts
4. Cooking
5. Sports

l know a man who is very interested in the Renaissance in Europe. He will tell you many interesting things that were a part of that time.

Pip Wilson, who works with inner city youngsters, says a good conversation starter with them is to ask them if they had a tattoo where would they have it and what would they have done!

My firm sent me on a computer course for a week. I became friendly with one of the other participants and discovered that he was quite an authority on World War II. The one evening we had off he drove me to a nearby aerodrome, now disused. I questioned him about the war. It was an evening I will never forget.

He told me about the dog fights that had been fought in the skies above us, what were the great assets of the Spitfires – and their limitations.

He was similarly knowledgeable about the Luftwaffe, and how Hitler had always seen its role as essentially a tactical one, to support the army in the field, and he never wished to have his bombers make raids on distant strategic targets such as ports, industrial cities and eventually residential areas.

He told me about the German experiments with

sophisticated long-range navigation, inspired by their famous Lorenz system of blind approach and landing.

Sometimes the best conversation starter is asking for advice. As a young man of twenty-six I bought a business. After a few months I saw I was going to make money. So I sought the advice of a well-known financier and two Christian businessmen. They all said the same thing – make personal and business budgets and keep within them, and open a savings account.

There was another thing both of the Christians emphasized, the importance of giving God back his portion. When you ask others for their counsel, you compliment them and come away a more informed person. Some cautions are:

1. Do not ask a doctor, lawyer, or other professional about a problem unless you are in the office and ready to pay for the advice.
2. Do not ask questions in a patronizing manner.

Use the person's name. People love to hear the sound of their own names. It makes them feel special that you took time to get it right and that you cared enough to personalize your comments. Do not, however, stick a name in indiscriminately, and do not overuse it.

When someone is interrupted, try remembering where departure from the main point occurred, and help bring the talk back to it. When you are at a loss for what to say or ask, remember the five W's: Who, What, Where, When, and Why.

Show genuine interest when something new comes into a person's life, such as a new car, furniture, vacation, wedding, baby, grandchildren, or job. Ask questions about the person's feelings concerning these things. What good is an achievement or a new possession if there is no one who is excited with you?

Above all, do not be a phony. Be a good listener and look for ways to be helpful. Get to know people better so that you may deal with them more knowledgeably when and if you get to the personalized spiritual area.

4

Another Ten Metres Nearer –
General Religious
Conversation

When you are ready to move on from the personal conversation level, it is time for God talk. Now you start filtering into the conversation religious topics such as church or youth group activities, or religious aspects of politics, like the ongoing Arab-Israeli conflict.

I heard of an evangelism team that went out on the street to witness. One of the questions they used as an icebreaker was, 'If you should die right now, could you say for certain you would go to heaven?' I would think that question, asked at that time and place, would be an ice*maker* rather than an icebreaker.

What I want to accomplish here is to start filtering into the conversation little 'seed thoughts' so I can eventually move to *personal* spiritual conversation. I want to bridge to that point and earn the right to ask personal spiritual questions. Just as I went from the general to personal conversation, I am now starting to bridge to the individual's religious life. I am using the word *religious* because that is what I talk about at this point. Although religion may be all he is familiar with at this point, in reality, I am bridging to the 'spiritual life.'

Over the years I must have listened to hundreds of sermons and talks by conference speakers. Some of the speakers, like Billy Graham, have now become very well-known. But I can still remember something that was said by Dr Walter Wilson. He was speaking on Psalm 126:6.

He said that we should have a 'leaky seed bag' over our shoulders so that wherever we go, seed will just spill out all over the ground.

That is what we should do in conversation once we have reached this point. There is no need to be obnoxious about it, but we can naturally bring God talk into conversations as the situations allow. When the person has reached the point in the process where the soil is fertile, he or she will respond in a more positive way.

Dr. Wilson illustrated 'dropping the seed' with his story of a young man working at a Sinclair gas station. Dr. Wilson drove into the station to get some gasoline. As the young man was filling his tank, Dr. Wilson said, 'I wonder how they will get the sin out of Sinclair.' The young man responded, 'I don't know, but I would like to know how to get the sin out of me.' With that, Dr. Wilson led him to Christ.

Have a Plan

Learn to do this seeding very strategically. Be able to sprinkle the gospel and spiritual life into a conversation tactfully. A football team will practice hour after hour on the field, practising shooting and dribbling, just so that they can get the ball past the opposing goal posts and into the net.

You must also be ready to give an account of the hope that lies within you (1 Peter 3:15). Take courses and read books on witnessing. Talk to knowledgeable people, read books, learn how to handle objections, know what to say to a JW or to an atheist. When God does bring you that one individual who is ready, you will be able to share Christ effectively. Be ready also to leave the spiritual talk and lead the conversation back into general topics if the situation warrants it, especially if the individual becomes antagonistic.

Dr. D. James Kennedy, founder of Evangelism Explosion, lists five main points as being foundational to the gospel:

1. Heaven is a free gift.
2. Man is a sinner.
3. God is just, so he must punish sin; but he is merciful, so he doesn't want to punish us, the sinners.
4. Jesus Christ, the infinite God-man, paid for our sins.
5. We must repent and trust in Jesus alone for our salvation.*

He uses this as a basic skeletal outline and adds 'flesh' to it with Scripture and illustrations. In my conversations with people I love to 'sprinkle in' these five points with their illustrations whenever possible. These are statements of value.

I have shared the whole gospel with people when they did not even know I was doing it. Even when I had not yet really earned the right to be 'up front' with someone, in order not to offend and still get the gospel across, I would do something like the following:

It is Easter. I allow Pat to drag me out to the

---

* D. James Kennedy, *Evangelism Explosion* (Wheaton, Ill.: Tyndale House Publishers, 1970), 21.

shopping centre. While she is enjoying herself going through the shops, I sit on a bench next to someone. I try to strike up a general conversation about how busy the place is. If he responds, I continue talking about the busyness, bringing up the time of the year. Then I point out how we have commercialized everything. Most of the time, he agrees. Then I say, 'It's too bad the way we are leaving the real values out of life. Here it is Easter and most of the women are more concerned about buying a new dress than they are that the Lord was raised bodily from a cold, dark grave to prove he was not a liar.'

That gets some attention! Using two words, *Lord* and *liar* together is not safe. Lightning might hit! What did I just bring out? Jesus Christ is God! That person just received a good blast of great doctrine. Witnessing can be so much fun! All this poor man is thinking about is how he is going to pay for the ham his wife bought for Sunday dinner. I come along and I am looking forward to heaven and the thousand-year reign with Christ and all of eternity.

I drop on this person the seed: Jesus is Lord! I have discharged my responsibility and am at peace with it. Whether or not he can handle it is not my responsibility. If he does show interest and responds to the gospel, I give him the whole plan of salvation and ask whether he would like to trust Christ right there. What an Easter that would be for him!

Do Not Feel Afraid or Spiritually Inferior

Why do we feel that people might think we are fanatics if we talk about God? This false assumption arises because we think that if all these people are not in our church or one just like it, then they do not respect or like God or things pertaining to God. That is nonsense!

There are millions of people who go to churches, temples, synagogues, and other houses of worship. Why do we assume they do not want to talk about their church or God or religious things?

There are many people who will talk about God and religion socially. Why should I pull away because of a few who are atheistic or agnostic? They, too, like to express their views on religion. They are just not sure how I will react to them. Will I get mad, lose my temper, or argue with them? Or do I have the confidence not to be threatened by their illogical arguments? Do I know what I believe and why I believe it?

There are two good books for those who are unsure about their faith. Both written by Paul E. Little, they are *Know What You Believe* and *Know Why You Believe* (see 'Suggested Reading').

Do I eagerly look for those who believe differently so I can love them and build inroads into their lives in order to earn the right to challenge their beliefs?

Why are we so hesitant? We have the answers to life and eternity through Christ. Christians have failed in not developing an attitude of humble confidence. We should not have a superior attitude, but rather one of 'thus saith the Lord.' We are saying to the unbeliever, 'Here it is. You are the one who decides to take it or leave it. You will have to live and die with your decision!'

We are not called to push the gospel on the

unbeliever. Beware of getting yourself in the position where you are force-feeding against someone's will. Just bring up the God talk and 'Those that have ears will hear.'

Jesus sometimes spoke in a sort of 'code' so that only 'insiders' would understand. Matthew 13 is an example. In verse 13 he says, 'This is why I speak to them in parables: Though seeing, they do not see; though hearing, they do not hear or understand' (NIV). In verse 15 he refers to their hearts as 'calloused.'

What is the point? Jesus was doing miraculous things, but people chose not to respond. All you can do sometimes is to present the God talk. If your hearers choose not to respond, there is little you can do to force them.

Also in Matthew 13 we find the parable of the sower. He sowed seed on four kinds of soil, but only one of the four soils produced a crop. As we get closer to the goal-mouth there will be fewer and fewer who will respond.

Basically, I see two main reasons why people do not always respond. First, they do not want to face their guilt. We have to be careful how we proceed here because people do feel guilty. Some psychologists say we should not feel guilt. Why not? If we are guilty, isn't it good that we feel guilty? Maybe then we will do something about it! One reason non-Christians drop out of conversations when we start to get close to their goal mouth is that they *are* guilty before the Lord and they are *feeling* it very strongly. So proceed very carefully.

Another reason they may not be responding is

because *we* may be trying to convict them, rather than letting the Holy Spirit work. Remember, we do not do the convicting, the Holy Spirit does. Simply share what you have. Before I learned some courtesy and know-how, I had some very negative encounters resulting in silence, crying, and tension. Just give the Word: God in his time will do the rest! Show a serving, loving, concerned attitude.

Bridges Into General Religious Conversation

Current events can often provide the conversational bridges into more religious talk. Here are some examples:

1. **Talk about the Israel-Arab conflict** and how that all started from biblical history. Many people have no idea of the biblical and historical backdrop to contemporary Middle Eastern conflicts.

2. **Talk about the decline of morals** and how God will judge a nation for its immorality. Refer to the problem of homosexuality and how that, although it is against nature, yet we are to love the homosexual with a Christ-like love. Mention the declarations on this subject in Romans 1.

3. **When someone mentions there is a wedding,** ask what church it is being held in. This may open opportunities to discuss theological differences and nuances between denominations.

4. **When someone moves into town,** ask if they have found the town hall, police station, tax office,

and the church of their choice. Simply by including the church in this list implies that choosing a church is a normal, expected thing to do when changing communities.

5. **Use God-related phrases** such as, 'Thank God' or 'God bless you.' Scripture says, 'out of the abundance of the heart the mouth speaks,' and such references are natural for one who knows God personally.

6. **Use different names or expressions for God.** First impressions are very important. In order not to come across as a religious fanatic, I will first lay the groundwork with certain laymen's terminology of God. Then I will move from that to the correct theological terminology. I do not want the person shutting me off, for it would then take a while to regain the ground I lost because of first impressions. When I think the situation calls for it, I will use the following names for God:

1. The Good Lord
2. The Lord
3. God
4. The Christ

After I think I have gained the person's confidence, I will use:

1. Jesus Christ
2. Christ
3. Jesus

It is a stair-step method. I take one step at a time

downward until I reach the landing below where the person is. I do not want to jump off the landing above and land on his head, knocking him to the floor in utter shock! Our goal is to lay the proper groundwork and then, in non-offensive but clearly understood language, to get across the following sequence of truths:

1. We are sinners and need to turn from our sin.
2. Christ died for us and shed his blood.
3. We must trust the Lord Jesus Christ.

Satan has done a good job of making the gospel message seem simple-minded! We must also battle against the image presented of preachers on television and on films, which often portray Christians as being somewhat odd. Many people will react as soon as we say anything about religion, and what we want is to be non-threatening. You do not want the hearer to shut you down mentally until you can share your message.

If, after you share, he still refuses it, then that is his decision. 'The natural man receiveth not the things of the Spirit of God; for they are foolishness unto him' (1 Corinthians 2:14). People rejected Christ during his time on earth and he will be rejected now, too. While we cannot avoid the offence of the Cross, we can exercise care so that people do not switch off before they have heard its message. We want to do everything in our power to show people their need to help them to turn to Jesus.

7. Use the holidays of Christmas and Easter as a springboard to conversation about the real reason for the season. People are more open to talk of spiritual matters at these times of the year. Public telling of the Christmas story, discussion of the text of Handel's *Messiah*, and other public holiday events may provide excellent springboard opportunities.

8. Share some personal spiritual truth. Opportunities often arise to personalize spiritual truth as we experience normal interaction with nonbelievers in the course of our ordinary working. For example, the scriptural teaching that one should not observe the Lord's Supper 'unworthily.' That concept may lend itself to the need either for confession, or for adherence to strict integrity in such issues as punctuality, being truthful at work, and not taking advantage of one's employer.

9. Use the other person's God talk as a bridge. Sometimes even at this early stage we can jump right in and head for the *personal* spiritual conversation. I read a very interesting article in a newspaper about a man who was the 'most accessible multi-millionaire.' The article reported that he owned a motel in Florida and that he accepted phone calls from anyone. It mentioned something about his belief in God, and that he hoped that when he died he would have peace. Well, that was all I needed!

I called information and obtained the phone number of the motel. On my second attempt, he answered. I complimented him on the article. After a few words (general to personal conversation), I mentioned what the article said about his faith and God. I shared with him how we can know for certain that we have eternal life (1 John 5:13). He told me he was not really interested in what I was saying because he was already doing enough to get to heaven. After I shared with him what the Bible says about works and heaven, he made another excuse or two.

I had done all I could. I thanked him for listening and being so approachable. I listed a few more Bible verses for him, just in case he cared to look them up later, and I hung up. The point of this illustration is that the *other person* brought up God. He made the move, and I just built from there. It is so much easier when the other person mentions religion or God first.

The same thing happened one time when I was in Milwaukee, Wisconsin, for a seminar. The speaker was talking to about eight hundred people. During this weekend seminar, he would mention God, but it was a god of the watered-down sort – the god in nature and mankind. I got up early one morning and checked the pool where he said he usually went during the first part of the day. Not finding him there, I sat in the lobby, hoping he would come through. It worked!

As he walked by, I asked for a private word with him. When he started to move to the side of the lobby with me, I explained that I would like to discuss a matter in the privacy of his room. I knew that if other people would see him, there would be interruptions. I told him that after ten minutes I would leave if he wanted me to.

We sat down in his motel room and I said, 'I have heard you speak of God several times during the sessions and I am very impressed. Most people do not mention God. What I would like to know is, what is your opinion concerning Jesus Christ?'

He became so engrossed in our discussion that he did not want me to leave. In fact, I stayed while he got ready for the next session. After about an hour of lively, insightful sharing, I left. During our talk he freely admitted to me that he needed to trust Christ and turn over his life to him. Although he did not do it at that time, the point remains that the gospel was shared without offending him.

Responding to Silence

When we do all this God talk and show these kindnesses, we sometimes feel our walk and words are not being noticed. When this thought haunts us, we can act or react in different ways:

1. We can feel guilty and press harder.
2. We can become discouraged and stop witnessing.
3. We can keep on with what we are doing, leaving the results to God.

The truth is, silent or not, people are noticing our witness. They just do not always show it or talk about it. We Christians notice good things about each other but say nothing. Why should a heathen, feeling guilty, tell you your witness is 'great?' Though he may not tell you the effect your witness has had on him, he will sometimes discuss it with his wife.

How do I know? Because people usually talk

about what happened during their day; especially those things that were different or out-of-the-ordinary. So here you are, sharing with them something during the week that they usually hear only on Sunday, and you are confident and excited about it.

Remember, my experience has shown that the nearer you get to the goal mouth, the fewer people there will be with whom you will get to share. With most people you are going to start a long way off, probably in your own half of the field. Once you start moving forward, people will start backing away and their defences go up. Accept that this is what happens. You bring up God talk and let them decide if you should continue.

Now let's move to personal religious comments.

5

Only Twenty-five Metres Out –
Personal Religious
Conversation

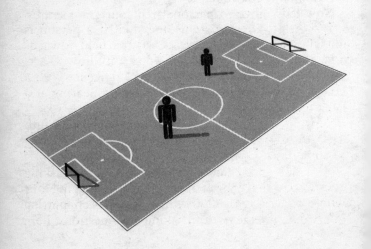

When you reach this far into a conversation, your objective is to see where an individual is in his personal religious life, so that you can lead into the gospel presentation when you reach the penalty box.

Some of the questions we should be asking are:

1. How far has God brought this person in the process?
2. Is he ready for the gospel? Is it time to bridge into the gospel presentation?
3. Be realistic. Is this what he wants? It is his decision. Do not try to force him.

It is helpful here to remember that if a person is not allowing you to move down the field towards him, the pressure is then off you. Withdraw. Tactfully change the subject. Reacting to reticence with a non-judgmental attitude may win you a hearing at a later time.

This idea of taking the general religious talk into the area of personal spiritual talk can be threatening to some.

As I have been talking to the person and asking questions, I have been moulding and shaping our whole conversation Godward. I have been putting out 'value statements' and asking key questions. I am now moving:

1. from general religious comments to specific spiritual comments (value statements).

2. from general religious questions to specific spiritual questions. I am now asking questions based on answers to my previous questions. I can now ask these more personal spiritual questions, for I have earned the right. At the beginning these questions are still general in nature: Where do you go to church? What does your church believe?

Then I ask what the person believes about specific spiritual subjects. I go from talking about God generally to talking about Christ specifically. I go from general morals to what the Bible actually says. I go from statements of fact and value to statements of personalization such as: God loves, God loves us all, God loves me, and, finally, God loves you!

Personalizing a private matter like a personal relationship to God is difficult. When moving into the personal religious area there are two things to bear in mind. Solicit your subject's personal views on different religious/spiritual subjects. This is transition, and it should be graceful.

Secondly, share with the individual – do not tell. Here Christians often come across as arrogant. I have found that what works best for me is not to make a statement but simply to ask a question. Example: I have talked about some church activity and the person has responded by either talking about his church or he has asked me more about the activity. I then ask him about his church and its teachings – that is if he is a church-goer. If I sense that he is open and that it is appropriate, I say something like, 'God wants to develop a personal fellowship with men.'

If he responds to that statement, I will ask, 'John, did you know that God wants to develop a personal fellowship with you?' Moving through these two transitions can be difficult for some people. It was for me.

I learned that just because I had progressed into the personal religious comments, I had not really arrived. I had to move the ball tactfully forward until I was in a position near enough to 'shoot for goal'. To be able to do this we must think through the ideas and concepts we are attempting to share. We must develop them in a progressive flow; one in which we are comfortable. We must constantly be building bridges not only from one major area to another, but also from metre to metre if necessary. This will take much of the clumsiness and fear out of witnessing.

John 4 (here paraphrased by the author) is the perfect example. Jesus was at Jacob's well when the Samaritan woman came to draw water. Jesus entered the 'personal' area immediately, saying to her, 'Give me a drink.' The woman responded with a question (smart lady). 'How is it that you, being a Jew, ask me for a drink since I am a Samaritan woman?' Jesus answered, 'If you knew the gift of God, and who it is who says to you, "Give me a drink," you would have asked him, and he would have given to you living water.'

Now Jesus has moved to the 'personal religious' area. She said to him, 'Sir, you have nothing to draw with and the well is deep; where, then, do you get this Living Water? You are not greater than our father Jacob, are you, who gave us the well and drank of it himself?'

I think she was confused at this point. That is why we must move slowly with people. She seemed to mix the 'personal' area ('You have nothing to draw with and the well is deep') with the 'general religious' area ('Where then do you get that Living Water?')

Jesus keeps moving toward the 'personal religious' talk with, 'Everyone who drinks of this water shall thirst again; but, whosoever drinks of the water that I shall give him shall never thirst, but the water that I shall give him shall become in him a well of water springing up to eternal life.'

The woman responded erroneously to what Jesus said. But she did respond. She said, in verse 15, 'Sir, give me this water, so I will not be thirsty, nor come all the way here to draw.' Because the woman was still responding, Jesus went to another area with which she needed to deal – her sin. Jesus said, 'Go, call your husband and come here.' What a powerful, wise, and tactful transition! She remained honest and responsive with Jesus by answering, 'I have no husband.' You see, before Jesus says, 'You have had five husbands and the one whom you now have is not your husband,' he has thrown out a question to bridge into this topic. He did not just bluntly raise the question of her sin. Jesus first put out a question to see her response, her openness to talk about the subject of her sin. As she responded, he progressed.

As I seek to direct a conversation toward the personal religious area, I am reading between the lines. I am listening for a heart attitude, but I must be careful not to be fooled by tears, thinking someone is seeking God when they are not. I must also be careful not to be fooled by a hard or gruff attitude which could be a cover-up. It could be God is working and that is why my subject portrays the gruff attitude!

I always have in the back of my mind the ultimate question: 'Do his actions and attitudes indicate that he wants me to proceed?' If I see rejection, or I do not see internalization of these personal spiritual matters, I pray and back off. If God, the Holy Spirit, does not bring these biblical truths home to the heart, there is no way I am going to be able to do so either.

Here are the reasons some Christians keep pushing ahead in spite of resistance:

1. They love the person and they want to share Christ, who is everything to them. But Christians who have loved ones who are unsaved have to learn to live with hurt. It hurts to see loved ones not trusting Christ. (See 'Learn to Live With Tension,' chapter 1).
2. They feel guilty if they do not push the gospel. If a person truly does not want to hear the message, it's time to back away. Remember that Christians are witnesses, not soul savers, and there is no guilt in tactfully withdrawing if defences are up. This may, in fact, win a hearing for the gospel another day.
3. Everyone loves to win at games. But soul winning should not be a one-upmanship game. 'I have to beat this person into sub-

mission and show him why he needs to be saved,' we often think. We are not to be headhunters, seeking only to earn stars for our crowns.

I remember going on a training course in evangelism. We were taken to a busy shopping precinct and told to use a religious questionnaire. I thought, 'Oh, no!' We would go through the religious questionnaire asking people the questions about God and religious beliefs. At the end of the questions, the questioner had one of two options: If the questioner felt the responses were hostile or indifferent, then he would thank the respondents for their time and move on. The second option was that if the people were open and 'into' the questions, the Christian would say something like, 'That completes the questionnaire. May I share something with you?' Then he or she would go into a presentation of the gospel.

Our trainer asked one couple the questions. But she did not ask to share with them. I asked her later why she chose not to share the gospel. She said she had picked up a hostile attitude in response to the questions. That was a good lesson for me.

When should one back away from presenting the gospel? In our personal spiritual talk, as we see we are getting reasonably close to the goal, 'value statements' of the gospel are sprinkled into the conversation in order to observe whether the listener is internalizing or personalizing the message. It can be observed much of the time. The message I am communicating in conversational style is:

1. Heaven is a gift – it is not earned or deserved.

2. Man is a sinner. Therefore he cannot save himself.
3. God is loving, but he is also just.
4. I state who Christ is and what he did.
5. I explain what faith is.

When I finish all this, I can tell 99 percent of the time whether I am to go further and present the gospel and ask for a decision. There is a fine line between talking about the gospel conversationally and sharing it personally. For me to go over that line can bring offence, and rather than spoil a later opportunity for witness it is often prudent for me to downplay pushing further.

It would be a travesty for me to offend someone due to my insensitivity, bad manners, lack of proper preparation, or inability to discern response to the gospel at this point. Personal offence is shameful; do not confuse it with the 'offence of the Cross' (Galatians 5:11), which refers to an unbeliever's negative reaction to the gospel message itself – not to the person who delivers the message.

This matter of backing away is a sensitive one. Many Christians press an unsaved person, feeling that if they do not, they are not being a good witness and are, in fact, denying the Lord. Backing away does not mean retreating all the way to your half of the field. It means going back to where the conversation was comfortable. We must not retreat in a reactionary manner. We still need to love, to pray, and to continue doing acts of kindness. We need to continue to be gracious, still letting the person know of our love by using reassuring statements.

What I am looking for is ripe fruit. Is he someone who has clearly been prepared by God? I can say all the right things, but he may not be ready. If I am in doubt about where he is, but he is still with me, I use a question I learned years ago. I use it two ways — first generally, then personally. The question is: 'John, did you know the Bible says we can know that we have eternal life?'

If he is still with me, I then personalize it with, 'John, did you know that you can know you are going to heaven?'

If he is *still* with me, then I go into the gospel presentation beginning with two other questions we will discuss later in this chapter.

We have to be careful here because at this point the lost person is deciding whether to listen to truth or not! This is where we start to do heart surgery. We are dealing with man's guilt, which is embarrassing and frustrating to him. Be careful, once again, not to offend. I understand a person's being offended by the gospel. That is between him and the Lord. But I do not want to be offensive by my method. I do not want him to be offended by me!

It is fantastic when you can observe the working of the Holy Spirit in a person's life. Someone may have already heard the gospel seven or eight times before, but you come along at God's right time, and enter the process. You build some bridges, present the opportunity, and a life comes to Christ!

The standard question to a person with whom you want to share the gospel is, 'If you were to die today, could you say for certain you would go to heaven?' Then ask, 'If you were to stand before God and he would ask, "Why should I let you into my heaven?" what would you say?' This second question lets you know what the individual is trusting in.

When I am getting to the edge of the penalty box I am asking these questions. How the individual answers these questions determines whether or not I shoot for goal with the actual gospel presentation.

6
**Shooting for Goal –
The Gospel
Presentation**

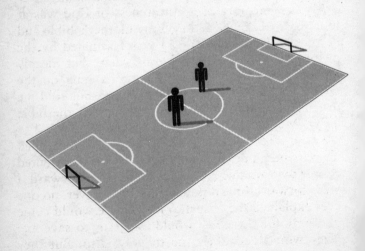

The gospel presentation should come from your own life. You are unique – one-of-a-kind! Your coming to Christ was an individual process. If you know nothing else, present that experience from a scriptural point of view. Think back. When was the first time you were 'God-conscious'? When was the first time you were aware of your sin? When did you realize that Christ died for you personally? What were the events that led up to your conversion? What were events that caused you to bow your head and trust Christ, confessing that you were a sinner?

My first memory of an awareness of God was at four years of age. I would get my mother's Bible and lie on the living room rug. I was fascinated by the picture of Daniel in the lions' den, but deeply disturbed by the picture of Christ hanging on the cross. I would ask my mother about it. She told me in later years that she would have to take the Bible away from me because I would get so upset.

Later, when I was nine or ten years old, I attended church and an evangelistic rally. The speaker invited people who wanted to 'get saved' to come forward. I went forward three different times. However, no one ever explained the gospel to me. People would come and pray for me. They would ask Jesus to save me. They would encourage me to pray, also. But they never explained the gospel!

After they had finished praying, I would go back to my seat. Dad would ask me what happened. I would tell him I got saved. What really happened to me was an emotional release that I mistook for salvation. I had not been told about my sinful nature. I did not understand Christ's role in the gospel. I was told to pray and ask Jesus to save me. Save me *from* what and *for* what? I didn't know.

I went to another evangelistic rally by myself as it was being held near my home. The speaker spoke over the time (about fifteen minutes) and I wanted to go home. At the invitation I noticed that people were walking to the front and then going out of the tent on the left. I decided I would get home sooner if I took this same route.

At the exit of the tent a fellow met me and asked if I wanted to get saved. I said, 'Yes.' This time the man sat me down, and with an open Bible shared with me what it really meant to be saved. He pointed out several verses about man's sin, that the Lord Jesus Christ died for me, and what I must do. It was the first time I remember someone going through the gospel logically with me. I started attending the church which had organised the tent meetings. My life took on real meaning, purpose, and direction.

When I first heard about a personal testimony, I really did not think mine was so unique. I did not have a sensational story to tell. I did not live a life of crime. I was just a very ordinary youngster, keen on football and cycling. But everyone's testimony is unique and will offer motivation to witness to others.

I am in favour of classes, books and training days which explain the how-to's of evangelism. But we are not talking of just head knowledge. The truth will come through the mind, but it must be believed in the heart. Our sharing Christ must be from the heart. That is what is going to speak to the hearts of others.

Different Methods

You may need to sharpen your witnessing skills. If you are a little timid or vague on some points of the gospel, then I recommend you attend some classes or seminars that will increase your knowledge. There are many methods. A few include:

1. SGM's 'Four things you should know'
2. Campus Crusade's 'Four Spiritual Laws'
3. Evangelism Explosion's 'five points'
4. The widely-used 'Bridge' illustration*

With all these you will find a specific number of points to share while presenting the gospel. Some have four parts and some have five, but they are all excellent presentations. Choose the method which best suits you.

To simplify the gospel to its basic truths, there are three things a person needs to know to become a Christian:

1. That man is a sinner
2. Who Christ is and what he did
3. That we must trust on the Lord Jesus Christ alone

If you were to come upon a deathbed scene and

---

* See 'Steps to Peace With God,' page 103.

the person was really wanting to go to heaven, and you did not know how much time he had left but you wanted to get the basic truths to him before he died, this is what he must believe.

Once a person expresses to me that he either wants to know how to go to heaven or he is open for me to share the gospel, then I begin tactfully telling him what the Bible says:

Man is a Sinner – Romans 3:23; 6:23
I turn in my Bible or his to Romans 3:23 and 6:23. I have him read it. I ask him questions: 'Bill, do you understand that man is a sinner and thus he is separated from God? Bill, do you understand that we are all sinners?'

Christ Died for Us – John 3:16
Then I might turn to John 3:16 and say, 'Bill, do you realize that Christ, the Son of God, died for you, so you can be saved?'

We Must Depend on Christ – John 3:16
Then I say, 'Bill, do you realize that you must trust in the Lord Jesus Christ alone in order to be saved?' If he says yes to all three questions, then I ask whether he would like to express to God his desires. I ask whether he would like to tell God that he realizes he is a sinner, that Christ died for him, and I ask if he would like to trust God right now.

This is an over-simplified example of a gospel presentation. But it shows how it can be done and also what is the content of the gospel. Whenever I think of learning any outline or gospel presentation, I think of what a famous actor once said about acting: 'A lot of rehearsing and memorizing goes on. I want to come across without letting the wheels show. The audience should see the play, not the actors.'

At times you may feel false or mechanical. But if you keep at your outline, keep practising, and keep remembering your unique experience of coming to Christ, then you will work through that feeling.

Life-Long Goal

Here is an extract from Josh McDowell and Don Stewart's book *Answers to Tough Questions*, which tells the story of the biblical scholar Robert Dick Wilson. It is a striking example of perseverance and should be an encouragement to us in our Christian endeavours:

The story of Dr. Robert Dick Wilson stands as a remarkable testimony to the reliability of the Bible. Wilson's scholarship, in many ways still unsurpassed, gave the world compelling evidence that the Old Testament is an accurate and trustworthy document. Robert Dick Wilson was born in 1856 in Pennsylvania. In 1886 Wilson received his doctorate. He continued his training at Western Theological Seminary in Pittsburgh, followed by two years in Germany at the University of Berlin.

Upon his arrival in Germany, Professor Wilson made a decision to dedicate his life to the study of the Old Testament. He recounted his decision: 'I was twenty-five then; and I judged from the life of my ancestors that I should live to be seventy; so that I should have forty-five years to work. I divided the period into three parts. The first fifteen years I would devote to the study of the languages necessary. For the second fifteen I was going to devote myself to the study of the text of the Old Testament; and I reserved the last fifteen years for the work of writing the results of my previous studies and investigations, so as to give them to the world.' Dr. Wilson's plans were carried out almost to the very year he had projected, and his scholastic accomplishments were truly amazing.

As a student in seminary he would read the New Testament in nine different languages including a Hebrew translation which he had memorized syllable for syllable! Wilson also memorized large portions of the Old Testament in the original Hebrew. Incredible as it may seem, Robert Dick Wilson mastered forty-five languages and dialects. Dr. John Walvoord, President of Dallas Theological Seminary, called Dr. Wilson 'probably the outstanding authority on ancient languages of the Middle East.'

Dr. Wilson commented on his scholastic achievements, relating why he devoted himself to such a monumental task: 'Most of our students used to go to Germany, and they heard professors give lectures which were the results of their own labours. The students took everything because the professor said it. I went there to study so that there would be no professor on earth that could lay down the law for me, or say anything without my being able to investigate the evidence on which he said it. . . .'

Wilson challenged other so-called experts in the Old Testament field demanding that they prove their qualifications before making statements concerning its history and text. 'If a man is called an expert, the first thing to be done is to establish the fact that he is such. One expert may be worth more than a million other witnesses that are not experts. Before a man has the right to speak about the history, the language, and the palaeography of the Old Testament, the Christian church has the right to demand that such a man establish his ability to do so.'

Dr. Wilson met his own challenge. For forty-six years Wilson had devoted himself to this great task of studying the Old Testament, carefully investigating the evidence that had a bearing upon its historical reliability. . . .

As a professor at Princeton, Dr. Wilson won international fame as a scholar and defender of the historic Christian faith. The emphasis of professor Wilson's teaching was to give his students 'such an intelligent faith in the Old Testament Scriptures that they will never doubt them as long as they live.' He tried to show them that there is 'reasonable ground for belief in the history of the Old Testament.'

What a remarkable story! I put it in a book on witnessing because it is such an example of dedication. If we Christians would take that attitude in our witnessing we could certainly accomplish much more for our Lord. We need to see the big picture, to keep ourselves motivated, and to have a goal of what there is to learn about evangelism. Do as Robert Dick Wilson did. Set up a schedule for the next ten, twenty, thirty years of what must be learned and done in order to become the best you can be at witnessing. There are five basic ways you need to prepare yourself to share the gospel:

1. **Practice sharing your personal testimony,** incorporating your own joy, personality, and the experiences through which God has brought you. Keep it

biblical and relatively brief – it should be an outflow of you. Do not present the Good News of Jesus Christ in a canned manner, but, rather, in a planned manner. Ask your pastor to listen to your presentation to be sure you have taken no liberties with the Scriptures. This way you will also be accountable to someone who will pray for you and encourage you to keep up your witnessing.

2. 'Hook' your testimony to the basic plan of salvation, using Scripture.

3. Learn how to give an answer from the Bible for: (*a*) people who think it takes works to get to heaven (church membership, baptism, giving money); (*b*) people who think it takes works plus grace; (*c*) people who think their sin cannot be forgiven; (*d*) people who do not believe in hell or that anyone really goes there.

4. Learn how to give answers from Scripture to the cults and their beliefs: (*a*) Jehovah's Witnesses deny the Trinity, the deity of Christ, the bodily resurrection of Christ, and the existence of hell and eternal punishment. They believe works earn man his salvation. (*b*) Mormons believe that God was once a man. They say men can achieve godhood. They believe the writings of Joseph Smith are divinely inspired revelations. They also believe that salvation is by works, and that man's multi-storied existence in heaven is determined by the scope of each man's good works. (*c*) Christian Scientists believe that God is merely an impersonal principle, that Jesus was not God, and that sin, evil, and death do not exist.

5. Learn how to answer – from Scripture – the beliefs of other world religions (i.e., Judaism, Hinduism, Buddhism, Islam, and Confucianism) concerning the uniqueness of Christ and Christianity.

Get to know all you can about Jesus from Scripture. Then when the cultist puts his wrong doctrine alongside the biblical Jesus, you can see it is false. This area of defending the faith is called apologetics – a defence. There are many great books written on apologetics, and when I am with an honest cultist, agnostic, or atheist, it is helpful to be able to quote from good resources on apologetics. But if you are dealing with a person who is closed in his thinking, all the arguments in the world will not change his views.

It is interesting that Paul, in the book of Colossians, refuted the philosophies and wrong teaching of his day by lifting up Jesus. He focused on the pre-eminence of Jesus, that he is above all and in all. He is supreme. Whenever I run across one of these people I just take them to Jesus. What do they think of Jesus? Is Jesus really God?

If they want to deal honestly with this issue, I will share with them gladly. But if they do not want to acknowledge Jesus as being supreme, then I have no more to say to them. Jesus is the keystone. That is the one argument in the area of apologetics I use: the 'trilemma' – Lord, liar, lunatic. Which one is he?

Some cultists, agnostics, or atheists will use the illogical argument that Christ is not God, but that he was a good man, great prophet, or teacher. C. S. Lewis said that calling Christ a great human teacher is patronizing nonsense. Logically, a person cannot take that position because of the claims of Christ. Christ claimed to be God! He is either God or some kind of liar or lunatic to make such a claim. I leave this argument with them. Let the Holy Spirit do the convicting.

We should never cease growing in Christ and his knowledge and wisdom. I believe most people get saved, grow for a year or so, and then live at that level of existence for the next thirty or forty years. How boring! If you have a desire to make disciples and to share Christ, then make this a lifelong goal. If a person wanted to begin playing a musical instrument, he would not want to take just a weekend mini-course or six weeks of lessons. He would commit himself to it, practice, and endure the discouraging times.

It is the same with disciple-making. There are setbacks, discouragements, and doubts. These are a part of the Cross Christ said we must pick up if we 'will' be his disciples. It is easy to be discouraged when people profess Christ but show no fruit — profession but not possession.

This book is intended to help you overcome subtle pitfalls in witnessing. Some things may be done in innocence, yet offend so much.

One of the things we need to learn about evangelism is that we make our mistakes on live people. When I say the wrong thing to someone or do not say the right thing, or when I go too far and make someone cry, that is when I feel like quitting.

But we also need to understand that when we make one of these mistakes, we have learned something, and, hopefully, we will never do that again.

God knows we were trying our best and he is patient while we are learning. He will use even our clumsy attempts for his glory. Do not think a person is lost for eternity because your presentation was poor.

I remember one wintry Thursday night. It was bitterly cold and windy and I had been out witnessing, getting doors shut in my face. I had been studying and memorizing outlines and Scripture. I had not eaten supper and I was tired. I would have much rather been home with my feet up, reading a good book. I had been in someone's home, had said the wrong thing, and had left as graciously as possible. Discouragement set in. I wanted to stop. But that is exactly what Satan wanted me to do. Part of being faithful is knowing we may make mistakes. We must look at the whole process and realize our part is to be diligent. View the whole evening as a time of your having been faithful, and do not focus on the mistakes. Do not give up. Keep on going. Practice! Practice! Practice!

7

Conclusion –
Witnessing:
Scoring the Goal

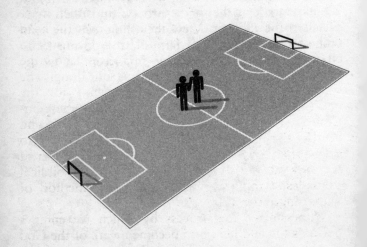

What we have in the back of our minds is very important when it comes to the pursuit of a goal or project. What we want to accomplish will come out in our motives, attitudes, and actions. If we get a proper biblical view of witnessing, then our concept of sharing the Lord Jesus will take on a whole new character.

I once saw a zealous young evangelist move right from 'kick off' into the attack. He went straight towards the other person who was still standing at the other end of the football field.

But nothing was going to stop this keen 'soul winner' from giving the gospel to the other man. With complete insensitivity, he hit him over the head with the Good News of Jesus Christ. He used no courtesy, no manners, nor was he aware of how the Lord was bringing this unsaved person along. The Christian felt the burden and the guilt for the unsaved person's lost soul. He felt that the non-Christian's blood would be upon his hands. 'The end justifies the means,' he rationalized. 'It is better to offend than to let one person go to hell.' However, if we look at the life of Christ and godly biblical examples, I think we would view this method of witnessing differently.

Witnessing is the process by which we enter a person's life and help him become aware of the God of the universe, Jesus Christ his Son, and of the sinner's need to align himself with his Creator and Lord.

Biblical witnessing is not a means to an end. The witnessing process is an end in itself. Witnessing is our goal, our 'end.' The whole football field is the witnessing area. Every metre we have to be a faithful witness. Witnessing is a serious commitment to invest in another human being's earthly growth and eternal destiny. That is why you must temper your approach to each person as you witness, being sensitive to his understanding based on life's experiences, his legitimate responses to your witness, and the working of the Holy Spirit in his life.

Keep in mind that God, the Holy Spirit, is not limited by our abilities. God is sovereign (Romans 9:19–24) and is not subject to any chart or football field method. These tools only help us humans know when to speak and when to be quiet.

Some people make no positive response to what you say and do not talk at all, while with others you may find yourself sharing the gospel within a few minutes, almost at their invitation. As you observe, experience, and feel the communication moving toward the goal mouth, you will soon become aware of the degree of openness your subject has to the gospel.

Experience has shown that most unsaved people do not know where they stand religiously. If you ask them the two questions at the end of chapter 5 regarding assurance of salvation and why they think they should go to heaven, they almost always give the wrong answers. They are trusting in the wrong things! If nothing else, that thought alone should motivate you to step out in faith and witness.

Be encouraged by Matthew 13:8–9, which says,

'But other seeds fell into good ground, and brought forth fruit, some a hundredfold, some sixtyfold, some thirtyfold. Who hath ears to hear, let him hear.'

A Typical Dialogue

The following is an illustration of a simplified presentation given to someone who is responsive and in whom the Holy Spirit is, and has been, working:

Bill: 'Hi, Joe. How are you today?'

Joe: 'I'm fine. How about you?'

Bill: 'Mustn't complain. Things are pretty good really. How was your Christmas?'

Joe: 'Great. The kids were all home, my wife excelled herself with her Christmas cooking, and we were able to get the things we really wanted this year. But, boy am I tired.'

Bill: 'Me too. This is such a busy time of the year in my business and personal life that it takes away some of the significance of the season.'

Joe: 'I know what you mean. I get tired of all the commercialism, too.'

Bill: 'What do you mean?'

Joe: 'Well, you know. All the overspending and running around surely does get monotonous year after year.'

Bill: 'It surely does. The whole meaning of Christmas gets lost, doesn't it?'

Joe: 'Absolutely.'

Bill: 'How do you observe the real meaning of Christmas, Joe?'

Joe: 'We all went as a family to one of these carols by candle-light services.'

Bill: 'Well, I'm really talking about something different. What I'm talking about is, what does Christmas mean to you personally?'

Joe: 'What do you mean?'

Bill: 'It's like this. Jesus Christ didn't come into the world just to form another religion. He came for the main purpose of dying and, Joe, he came to die for you and me personally.'

Joe: 'I know he died for the whole world.'

Bill: 'That's true, Joe. The Bible says that. But where this becomes significant is in knowing he died for you personally, so that you can go to heaven when you die.'

Joe: 'You know, I have an aunt who talks about God like you do.'

Bill: 'Has anyone else ever talked to you personally about God?'

Joe: 'Yes, I've a friend at work named Don who talks this way about, God, too.'

Bill: 'Joe, to help clarify the whole meaning of Christmas as it relates to you, could I ask you a question?'

Joe: 'Sure.'

Bill: 'If you were to die right now, could you say for sure you would go to heaven?'

Joe: 'I hope so.'

Bill: 'Let me ask you another question. If you were to die and stand before God, and he were to ask you, "Why should I let you into my heaven?" what would you say?'

Joe: 'Well, I do the best I can. I'm not a bad guy. I'm a good husband and father and I think I'm as good as most of the people who go to church.'

Bill: 'Let me share with you what the Bible says is required to go to heaven. First of all, the Bible says we are all sinners (Romans 3:23), "For all have sinned and come short of the glory of God." Then Romans 3:10–11 tells us, "As it is written, there is none righteous, no, not one . . . there is none that seeketh after God." These verses point out that not only has man offended God in the general sense, but we specifically have offended God. I have offended God, and you have offended God. The question I want to ask you is, do you understand that?'

Joe: 'I'm afraid I do.'

Bill: 'Do you know what the consequences are for your sin?'

Joe: 'No.'

Bill: 'Joe, read this verse (Romans 6:23).'

Joe: ' "For the wages of sin is death, but the gift of God is eternal life through Jesus Christ our Lord." '

Bill: 'Joe, do you understand what that death in the verse is?'

Joe: 'It probably means when I die.'

Bill: 'No, it is speaking of spiritual death, separation from God for all eternity – hell. What the Bible is saying is that because we are sinners, when we die, we will go to hell! But, now, here is the Good News. Christ died for us! Continuing with the verse, "But the gift of God is eternal life through Jesus Christ our Lord." Christ's death satisfied God's anger toward sin. Joe, your responsibility is to depend on Christ alone to be saved from this death and go to heaven. Let's turn to Acts 16:30–31. Read it out loud.'

Joe: ' "And he brought them out, and said, 'Sirs, what must I do to be saved?' And they said, 'Believe on the Lord Jesus Christ, and thou shalt be saved.' " '

Bill: 'The man asked Paul what he needed to do to be saved. Paul told him what he had to do. Joe, what did he have to do?'

Joe: 'Believe on the Lord Jesus Christ.'

Bill: 'Do you believe Christ will save you if you ask him to?'

Joe: 'Sure.'

Bill: 'Would you like to do that right now?'

Joe: 'Yes, I would.'

Bill: 'Do you want to pray and confess to God that you are a sinner and ask him to save you? Does this express what you want to do?'

Joe: ''Yes.'

(At this point Bill leads Joe in prayer.)

Bill: 'Now, if you were standing before God and he asked you why he should let you into his heaven, what would you say?'

Joe: 'Because he died for me and I asked him to save me.'

Bill: 'That's right! If you were to die right now, Joe, do you know for sure you would go to heaven?'

Joe: 'Yes!'

Bill: 'Why?'

Joe: 'Because I believe that Christ saved me.'

Follow up to confirm his assurance of his decision with the same two questions in reverse. His answers declare his understanding, whether or not he knows what he did. If he is unsure, take him back to the verses. If he is sure, you will know by his answers. This procedure follows what is taught by D. James Kennedy in his Evangelism Explosion seminars.

A Final Challenge

As you go about your daily living, ask God to give you opportunities to reach the lost by fitting into his design for each person's life.

If you are doing your job of effective witnessing, you will find there a surprising number of people you can talk to about the Lord Jesus Christ. To use our football analogy for the last time, for many you will not be able to progress very far down the field, but some will have been waiting for you to 'shoot for goal'.

Your success is not determined by where others are in the process. Your success, before God, is based on your obedience to his command to share as you go. Simply put, successful witnessing is . . . taking the initiative to share Christ in the power of the Holy Spirit . . . and leaving the results to him.

Suggested Reading

Lewis, C.S. *Mere Christianity*. Fontana, 1970.

Little, Paul E. *Know What You Believe*. Scripture Press, 1987.

Little, Paul E. *Know Why You Believe*. Scripture Press, 1987.

Martin, Walter. *The Kingdom of the Cults*. Bethany House Publishers, 1977.

When They Come Knocking. Leaflet. CLF, 1991.

McDowell, Josh & Stewart, Don. *Answers To Tough Questions Sceptics Ask About the Christian Faith*. Tyndale, 1980.

McDowell, Josh. *Evidence That Demands a Verdict*. Here's Life Publishers, 1979. UK edition: Scripture Press.

McDowell, Josh. *The Resurrection Factor*. Here's Life Publishers, 1981. UK edition: Scripture Press.

Morison, Frank. *Who Moved the Stone? InterVarsity press, 1969. UK edition: Send the Light Trust.*

Packer, J.I. *Evangelism and the Sovereignty of God*. InterVarsity Press, 1961.

Pippert, Rebecca Manley. *Out of the Salt Shaker and Into the World*. InterVarsity Press, 1979.

Ridenour, Fritz, editor. *So What's the Difference?* Regal Books, 1967.

Steps to Peace With God

STEP

1 GOD'S PURPOSE: PEACE AND LIFE

God loves you and wants you to experience peace and life — abundant and eternal.

The Bible says...

"...we have peace with God through our Lord Jesus Christ." Romans 5:1

"For God so loved the world that He gave His only begotten Son, that whoever believes in Him should not perish but have everlasting life." John 3:16

"...I have come that they may have life, and that they may have it more abundantly." John 10:10b

Since God planned for us to have peace and abundant life right now, why are most people not having this experience?

STEP

2   OUR PROBLEM: SEPARATION

God created us in His own image to have an abundant life. He did not make us as robots to automatically love and obey Him, but gave us a will and freedom of choice.

We chose to disobey God and go our own wilful way. We still make this choice today. This results in separation from God.

The Bible says...
"For all have sinned and fall short of the glory of God." Romans 3:23

"For the wages of sin is death, but the gift of God is eternal life in Christ Jesus our Lord." Romans 6:23

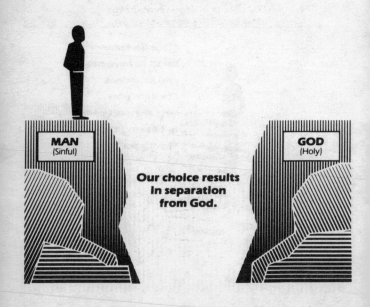

MAN
(Sinful)

GOD
(Holy)

**Our choice results
in separation
from God.**

Our attempts...

Through the ages, individuals have tried in many ways to bridge this gap...without success...

The Bible says...

"There is a way that seems right to a man, but in the end it leads to death." Proverbs 14:12

"But your iniquities have separated you from God; and your sins have hidden His face from you, so that He will not hear." Isaiah 59:2

There is only one remedy for this problem of separation.

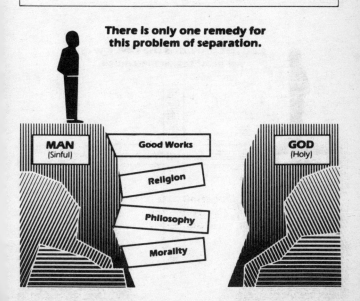

MAN
(Sinful)

Good Works

Religion

Philosophy

Morality

GOD
(Holy)

STEP

3

GOD'S REMEDY: THE CROSS

Jesus Christ is the only answer to this problem. He died on the Cross and rose from the grave, paying the penalty for our sin and bridging the gap between God and man.

The Bible says...

"...God is on one side and all the people on the other side, and Christ Jesus, Himself man, is between them to bring them together..." 1 Timothy 2:5

"For Christ also has suffered once for sins, the just for the unjust, that He might bring us to God..." 1 Peter 3:18a

"But God demonstrates His own love for us in this: While we were still sinners, Christ died for us." Romans 5:8

**God has provided the ONLY way...
we must make the choice...**

MAN
(Sinful)

CHRIST

GOD
(Holy)

STEP

4

OUR RESPONSE: RECEIVE CHRIST

We must trust Jesus Christ and receive Him by personal invitation.

The Bible says...

"Behold, I stand at the door and knock. If anyone hears My voice and opens the door, I will come in to him and dine with him, and he with Me." Revelation 3:20

"But as many as received Him, to them He gave the right to become children of God, even to those who believe in His name." John 1:12

"...If you confess with your mouth the Lord Jesus and believe in your heart that God has raised Him from the dead, you will be saved." Romans 10:9

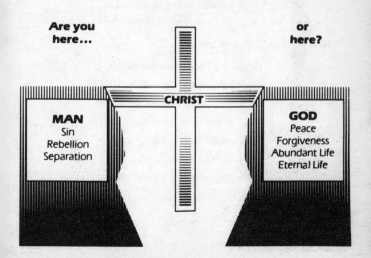

Are you here...

or here?

CHRIST

MAN
Sin
Rebellion
Separation

GOD
Peace
Forgiveness
Abundant Life
Eternal Life

Is there any good reason why you cannot receive Jesus Christ right now?

How to receive Christ:

1. Admit your need (I am a sinner).
2. Be willing to turn from your sins (repent).
3. Believe that Jesus Christ died for you on the Cross and rose from the grave.
4. Through prayer, invite Jesus Christ to come in and control your life through the Holy Spirit. (Receive Him as Lord and Saviour.)

WHAT TO PRAY:

Dear Lord Jesus,

I know that I am a sinner and need

Your forgiveness. I believe that You died

for my sins. I want to turn from my sins.

I now invite You to come into my

heart and life. I want to trust You as

Saviour and follow You as Lord, in

the fellowship of Your church.

Date _____   Signature _____

GOD'S ASSURANCE: HIS WORD

If you prayed this prayer,

The Bible says... "For 'whoever calls upon the name of the Lord will be saved.'" Romans 10:13

Did you sincerely ask Jesus Christ to come into your life? Where is He right now? What has He given you?

"For it is by grace you have been saved, through faith — and this is not from yourselves, it is the gift of God — not by works, so that no one can boast." Ephesians 2:8,9

The Bible says... "He who has the Son has life; he who does not have the Son of God does not have life. These things I have written to you who believe in the name of the Son of God, that you may know that you have eternal life, and that you may continue to believe in the name of the Son of God." 1 John 5:12-13

Receiving Christ, we are born into God's family through the supernatural work of the Holy Spirit who indwells every believer...this is called regeneration or the "new birth."

This is just the beginning of a wonderful new life in Christ. To deepen this relationship you should:

1. Read your Bible every day to get to know Christ better.
2. Talk to God in prayer every day.
3. Tell others about Christ.
4. Worship, fellowship, and serve with other Christians in a church where Christ is preached.
5. As Christ's representative in a needy world, demonstrate your new life by your love and concern for others.

God bless you as you do.

Billy Graham